1

Gary walked up a dark lane to the railway station in Diss. It was a frosty December evening. His face felt stiff and chilled by the cold, like a mask. He was used to driving everywhere and had not brought an overcoat or gloves. He had forgotten how cold you could feel on a winter's night.

He looked at his watch. It was five minutes past nine. The Inner-City train from London was not due for another ten minutes.

It had been a while since he caught a train. Gary thought, as he walked into the empty station. He worked in Norwich as an insurance salesman and spent most of his day driving to meetings. But that afternoon he had left his car in the city to be serviced. A friend had given him a lift to an evening meeting in Diss. Gary had been unable to find a lift home, so he had had to take the train back.

He walked to the edge of the platform. As a child he used to feel excited standing so close to the track when the trains rushed by. It was like standing by the side of a fast river, just one step away from death. That sounded like a good title for one of the thrillers he liked to read, he thought. He had one in his briefcase. He spent his days selling life insurance and felt the need for some excitement in his life.

Gary looked down at the clean silver rails on the dark bed of cinders. In the light from the platform, the steel of the rails looked cold and polished. Just beyond the end of the platform was the white wooden signal box. It was a bright cage of light in the darkness. It looked warm inside.

Somewhere down the track Gary could hear a signal lift and click. Gary heard the rails begin to shiver and ring by his feet. The train must be close, he thought. He really ought to stand back from the edge of the platform, he knew that. But somehow he wanted to feel the excitement as the train rushed in.

Sooner than he thought, the train swept in, making Gary catch his breath. As the train stopped, he looked through the windows for a seat. There were plenty to choose from. In fact, the train looked almost empty.

Gary opened a door. The handle felt icy cold in his fingers. People were saying it would snow before the end of the week. Gary opened the door of the train. He would be glad to be in out of the cold.

2

Inside the train, the empty compartment was warm, but the air felt stale. After the one and a half hour trip from London Diss was the last station before Norwich. Most of the passengers had probably left The train at earlier stops, Gary thought.

On the tables there were empty crisp packets and coffee cups. Newspapers lay tired and crumpled on seats. Gary's foot kicked an empty beer can as he walked up the aisle. He felt like a guest arriving at a party that had just finished.

He sat down in a seat by a window. The train moved off slowly. The lights of Diss station slid by as the train headed off into the darkness of the December night.

Gary settled into his seat. He picked up a ring-pull from a drink can and began to play with it in his fingers. He could not see far into the darkness outside. By the track the dark ditches and black winter trees rushed by in the light from the train windows.

Gary began to feel tired. He decided not to read his book. It had been a long day. He rested his head back against the seat. It would be nice to sleep most of the way to Norwich.

Suddenly the lights dimmed as the train shuddered to a halt. Gary sat up quickly. Outside in the darkness there was a flash of pale blue light from above the train. Gary looked up as the lights brightened again in the train. There must be something wrong with the overhead wires, Gary thought. Perhaps there was ice on the cable.

Gary was settling back into his seat when the compartment suddenly fell into complete darkness. Outside, there were several electric blue flashes from above the train. With each flash Gary could see far out over the flat fields. For an instant the marshland was drenched in a blue ghostly light. Gary stared out. It was a strange sight.

Then something in the pale blue landscape caught his eye. Gary leaned forward quickly in his seat. On a road next to the railway track Gary thought he saw a car stop suddenly under a tall tree by an old windmill. He saw a man thrown out of the car into a

ditch. Then the marshland fell back into darkness again.

Gary waited for another blue flash. Yes, there was the car. And the body. From the angle of the man's neck, Gary could see he was dead. Then the scene vanished into the darkness as the lights in the carriage came on and the train started moving again.

Gary leaned back in his seat. He felt shocked. Part of him could not believe what he had seen. A dead man thrown from a car into a ditch.

Gary looked around the bright compartment. Everything was the same. The coffee cups. The London newspapers. Then he looked down at his hands.

In the shock of seeing the dead body he must have gripped the ring-pull in his fingers. The metal had cut cleanly into his thumb. Blood trickled down into the palm of his hand.

Gary lifted his hand to his mouth to suck the cut thumb. He could feel his hand shaking. In fact, he could feel himself shaking all over. Mostly with fear. He had not seen a dead body before. But he also felt a strange excitement.

Gary wondered if he had been a witness to a murder.

3

Gary paid the taxi and walked up Lime Avenue to his house. In the light of the street lamps the windscreens of the parked cars were grey with frost. Gary looked at his watch. It was after midnight. He had just spent an hour in the police station.

At the front door, Gary's hands were so cold he found it hard to fit the little Yale key in the door-lock. He put the fire on in the living-room and went into the kitchen to make some tea. He wanted to relax and get warm before he went to bed. He still felt tense and excited. It was not every night He gave a statement to the police about a murder. It was like being in one of the detective stories he read.

He lit a gas-ring on the cooker and looked down at the neat little crown of pale blue flames. The pale blue was almost the same as the strange light from the electric flashes of the train. Gary made the tea and walked into the living room.

He did not bother to put the light on. He went and sat in an armchair by the orange light of the gas-fire. His black cat, Ben, walked in from the cold kitchen and lay one the warm hearth rug, stretched out on his side like a lion.

Gary looked down at the cat. Ben was an old stray he had taken in. He had been in some backyard fights in his time and had the scars to show for it. One eye was always half shut. The edge of his left ear was clipped and nicked.

Gary's thoughts went back to the train ride home. He felt the police officer had not really believed him when he told him what he had seen from the train. But they would have to believe him when they went and found the body.

Ben jumped up on to the arm of the chair and pushed against his hand. He had not seen Gary all day and wanted to be fussed over. Gary put his cup of tea to one side and stroked Ben's head. The cat's ears folded softly like felt against his hand. Ben purred.

Gary began to relax. He felt he could fall fast
asleep, just sitting there in the darkness with Ben in
front of the warm fire. If he stood up to go to bed,
he knew he would only feel wide awake again.
It was always the same. He would lie awake for
hours in bed, thinking about work.

It seemed as if he had only been asleep for a
moment when he sat up quickly in his chair.
He had had a strange dream.

In the dream he had seen a hand raised above a
man's chest. It held something sharp and silver, like
a knife. The hand came down quickly three times
across the man's chest. One. Two. Three.
Then he saw the white car and the dead body in the
ditch by the old windmill.

For several moments Gary sat in his chair, shocked
by the dream. He kept seeing the flash of silver in
the hand as it stabbed down on the chest.

Gary looked around the dark room. All was quiet.
He could feel the soft heat from the gas fire against
his legs. On the video recorder the figures on the
clock glowed a bright green in the darkness.

Yes, it had only been a dream. What he had seen from the train window must have given him quite a shock. He should have gone straight to bed instead of dozing in the chair.

Gary looked around the room for Ben. He had felt him jump from his lap to the floor when he had woken up suddenly from the dream. He was surprised to see Ben hiding under the settee. He stared out at Gary. His ears were flat down against his head. Along his neck and back the black fur was stiff with fright.

Gary tried to coax him out from under the settee. But it was no good. After while, Gary gave up and went to bed.

Ben still stared out from under the settee. His one green eye had a wild look. Gary had never seen him so frightened before.

4

The next morning Gary was late up. He had slept badly. He had had another dream about the dead body in the ditch. As he woke up, the dream was still running in his head. There was the white car, the hand with the knife, and the body in the ditch by the old windmill. But there had been other details in the dream too. Gary sat on the side of his bed and tried to remember what they were.

A strange set of numbers seemed to be part of the dream. He wondered if they made up the number plate of the car. He could not remember seeing many letters. It was mostly numbers, like on a French number plate. There was 41, then 29, and then a 2, or was it a Z or an S? At the back of his mind Gary felt there was something else about the car, but he could not quite remember what it was.

Gary picked up his watch from the bedside table. He looked at the time. He had to hurry, as he had to pick up his car before he went to work. He did not have time to sit and think about dreams.

Gary dressed quickly. As he sorted out a tie to wear, he thought about how he would tell the people at work about what had happened. It was quite a story. He would be the talk of the office.

He decided he would tell Helen first. Helen was the new girl in the accounts department. She had only started at the office two weeks ago. Gary liked her and was always finding excuses to go and talk to her.

Most mornings he found himself telling her about the latest detective story he was reading. Gary thought they seemed to be getting on well. Well, he would have a great story to tell her that morning, he thought and smiled. He took his time picking out the smartest tie to go with his best jacket. Perhaps when the papers got hold of the story, they would want his picture.

Gary walked down the stairs to the kitchen. His mind went back to the dream. He was trying to Remember the other detail about the car.

Gary looked up at the clock. It was twenty past eight. He would have to leave before nine to pick up his car, so he would not have time to catch the news. If the police had found a body, he was sure it would make the headlines of the local news programmes on the radio.

Gary went over to the sink the fill the kettle. He did not have time for much breakfast, just a quick cup of coffee. He reached for the hot tap. It would take less time to boil if he put in hot water. He turned the tap on. The gas boiler on the wall switched itself on and began to roar loudly.

As Gary filled the kettle, the other detail in the dream suddenly came back to him. The roar of the boiler had reminded him of the sound of the car engine in the dream. It had sounded rough and loud, like a sports car.

Gary turned the tap off and went to find his coat. He could do without the coffee. What he wanted now was news about the murder. He was sure a foreign car was involved. And he felt certain it was a sports car.

5

Gary caught a bus into the city and then walked quickly to the garage where his car had been serviced.

In the garage showroom, bright winter sunlight fell through the wide windows. The chrome trim on the cars shone silver in the sunshine. Gary looked at his watch. It was ten to nine. If he could get his car in time, he could listen to the nine o'clock news bulletin on the radio.

Gary knew the staff in the garage, so he walked through some swing doors into the workshop at the back.

After the bright sunlight of the warm showroom the workshop was dark, like a cave. The air tasted of oil and petrol. Somewhere a radio was playing music. Gary liked garage workshops. Like most people who didn't have to work in one, Gary thought working in a garage looked interesting.

On a wall a long rack of ring spanners hung in all
sizes. From under the bonnet of a car he could hear
the quick ticking of someone working a ratchet
wrench. At the back, in the darkness, the pale blue
star of a welding flare burned brightly.

Gary called out to Steve. Steve turned the welding torch down.

It burned for a moment with weak yellow rags of flame and then died. Steve came over and began to talk to Gary about his car. Gary was not really listening. He was looking at his watch.

'Sorry, Steve, I'll have to go. Not much time this morning. If you can just let me have the keys, I'll call back and pay the bill later. You haven't had a chance to hear the local news today, have you?'
'No, I haven't. I've been at work since seven o'clock. Unlike some people I know,' Steve said and smiled. Like most people who didn't have to work in one, Steve thought working in an office was easy.

Back in his red Escort, Gary started the engine and turned on the radio. He looked at the clock on the dashboard. It said 8.55. He set off for his office in the city. There was so much traffic it would take him half an hour, he thought.

As he drove, he began to feel tense. He wondered if there would be something on the nine o'clock news about the dead body. He thought back to the strange dream last night, the body, the stabbing, the numbers and the sporty engine. Did it mean anything at all? Or was it all just a dream?

Gary looked out at the long queue of traffic leading into the city. He looked down at the clock. It was one minute to nine.

Up ahead there was a large roundabout. In the middle of the roundabout stood an electricity pylon, like a tall grey iron cage. As he moved slowly towards it, the radio began to crackle.
He could hardly hear the bleeps of the time signal as the nine o'clock news started. Gary tried to tune into a stronger signal, but it was no good. There was so much interference he could hear none of the news.
Gary gave a tense laugh and shook his head.
If it wasn't all happening for real, he would think he was in the middle of a thriller of some sort.
Still, it would all make a good story to tell at work.
He turned off the radio and put in a tape.
He hardly ever drove without music of some sort.

When he arrived at work, he went straight to his office to ring the police. One way or another he wanted to know what they had found.

6

Gary put the phone down. The police had found nothing, they said. They had searched all the way along the roads by the railway track and found nothing. He could not believe it. They must have gone to the wrong spot, he thought.

Gary was sitting by the window of his office. Through the bare twigs and branches of a tall tree he could see a cold blue winter sky. Over to the west there was a bank of low dark cloud. Gary was trying to decide whether to go and look along the roads by the railtrack for himself. I'll go and ask Helen's advice, he thought. He couldn't wait to tell her the whole story.

Helen's office was a strange place, Gary thought, as he went in. All the staff worked at computers and kept the blinds drawn so that the VDU screens were brighter and easier to see. Even in the middle of the day most of the room was dark. Here and there desk lamps were lit, making little pools of light in the darkness, like a nightclub.

Gary sat on Helen's desk beside her computer. He began to tell her about the train ride home last night. She carried on typing figures from a pile of yellow invoices by her side. Why, she wondered, did Gary always have to bore her with his odd stories?

She was new to the office and she worried that her supervisor might see her not working.

She kept her eyes fixed on the papers by her side. She stopped suddenly when she heard about the dead body and the detail about the stabbing. She looked up at Gary.

'Are you sure this isn't one of those stories you're always reading, Gary?'

'No, Helen. This is for real,' Gary said. 'I'm sure there is a sports car involved too.'

'Why a sports car?' Helen asked.

'Well, in the dream the car had a loud engine noise. It had a rough, racy, sporty sound. It was really loud. And there was something else too,' Gary said. He waited a moment. He could see Helen was interested. He was enjoying being the centre of attraction.

'I'm sure it was a foreign car. In the dream I kept seeing this strange number plate. It was something like 41 92 2.'

'Did you fill in a week's invoices before you went to bed, Gary?' Helen asked and laughed.

Gary gave her a puzzled look. 'Yes, I did actually. I couldn't sleep, so I did some paperwork sitting up In bed. Why do you ask that?'

'Well. Those numbers are yesterday's date. Today is the 5th December. Yesterday was the 4th. The 4th of the 12th, you see. 4. 12. 92. You had probably written it a dozen times on your invoices. Since I started here, I have figures going round in my head most nights!'

Gary looked away. All of a sudden he felt a little silly. What Helen had said was true. It could just have been a date from an invoice. Perhaps the dream was nothing more than that, just a dream.

'But then what about the car and the dead body?' Gary said quickly. 'Don't forget I actually saw them. That was no dream. I was thinking I might drive out there myself this afternoon and try to find the place where it happened. I'm sure I would recognise it again if I saw it.'

'Yes. I'm sorry, Gary. I didn't mean to make a joke
out of the whole thing.' Helen could see that he
looked hurt. She began to feel sorry for Gary.
She quite liked him in a way. He was one of the few
people who had had time for her in her first days at
the office. It was just that he was such a bore with
his detective stories. And he was always so badly
dressed too. Just look at him now, wearing a brown
tie with a dark blue suit, she thought.

Helen suddenly saw that her supervisor was looking
in their direction. She said quickly, 'Look, Gary.
Why not forget all about it? You've told the police.
Why not just leave it all in their hands?'

'Yes. I'm sure you're right, Helen.'
But he was only being polite. As he left her office,
he was already feeling in his pocket for his car keys.

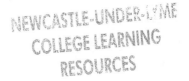

7

As Gary walked out to his car, he wondered if Helen
was right. Perhaps he ought to leave it in the hands
of the police. But then they had said they had found
nothing. Perhaps they had not looked along the right
stretch of road. Or they might never have gone to
look for the body at all. He felt the police officer
had not really believed him anyway.

And he was sure that Helen didn't believe half of what
he had told her. As Gary opened the car door, he
decided to make two business calls in Norwich first
and then drive straight down to Diss. He did not know
what he would find, but he would prove them all
wrong somehow. Gary knew there was a body waiting
there to be found. And he knew he had his part to play.

Gary was held up at his last business call and did not
leave Norwich for Diss till just after two o'clock. He
drove quickly out of the city into the countryside. On
the skyline, bare winter trees stood out against a cold
blue sky. Low winter sunlight shone on the water in
the long straight ditches that crossed the marshland.

Just outside Diss, Gary turned off the main road and began to work his way through back roads towards the railway line out of the town.

He drove quickly. He knew he did not have much time. It was December and it would start to get dark early. Over in the west a ridge of low grey clouds was beginning to close over the marshland.
He turned the radio off so that he could think back to where he had seen the white car the night before.

Gary stopped and got out of the car. He climbed the bank by the road and looked over a hawthorn hedge. Just across the frosty fields lay the railway line. And yes, there it was. About a mile down the road, Just on a bend, stood a tree by an old windmill.

Gary scrambled down the bank and jumped into the car. As he drove away quickly in first gear, he noticed the car engine had an odd sound. With the radio on he had not noticed it before. It sounded rough and noisy. He suddenly remembered something Steve had said that morning in the garage. Something about a hole in the exhaust.

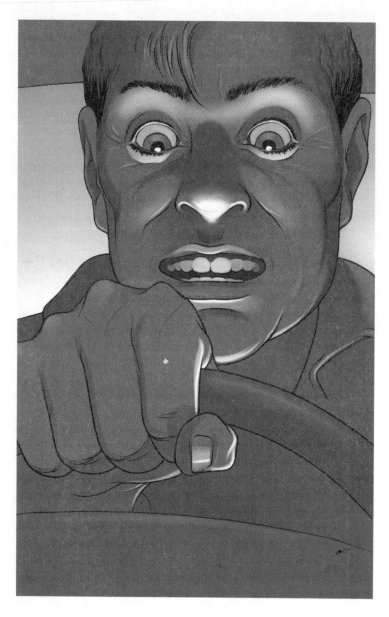

As he reached down to put the car into second gear, He felt his seat belt unclick. In his rush to drive away he had not put it on properly. It began to slip up over his chest. He reached across with his left hand and tugged the shiny silver buckle down sharply. It jammed. He tugged it down again across his chest, and again. It jammed each time.

As he pulled on the buckle, he lost control of the car on the icy bend. His arms stiffened against the impact of the crash as the red Escort spun into the bank under the tree. His eyes stared wildly at the reading on the mileage clock. It was 41,292.

The sound of the crash faded quickly in the silence of the empty marshland. Soon the sun had set, and the long lanes of sunlit water in the ditches turned grey and cold. The bank of heavy, low cloud moved in from the west and closed over the flat landscape like a dark wing.

After a while it began to snow. When a man on a passing train spotted the wreckage, the car he saw was white.